Sindbad the Sailor

Retold by N. J. Dawood

Adapted by Cherry Gilchrist

Level 3

Series Editor: Melanie Williams

Pearson Education Limited
Edinburgh Gate, Harlow
Essex CM20 2JE, England
and Associated Companies throughout the world.

ISBN 0582 512573

This adaptation first published by
Penguin Books 2003

3 5 7 9 10 8 6 4

Text copyright © Penguin Books 2003
Illustrations copyright © A.McBride/Linden Artists and B.Dowty/GCI (page 31)

The moral rights of the author and illustrator have been asserted

Design by Wendi Watson
Colour reproduction by Spectrum Colour Limited, Ipswich
Printed in China SWTC/03

Published by Pearson Education Limited in association with Penguin Books Ltd,
both companies being subsidiaries of Pearson Plc

For a complete list of the titles available in the Penguin Young Readers series
please write to your local Pearson Education office or to:
Penguin Readers Marketing Department, Pearson Education,
Edinburgh Gate, Harlow, Essex CM20 2JE

Contents

Sindbad's First Journey

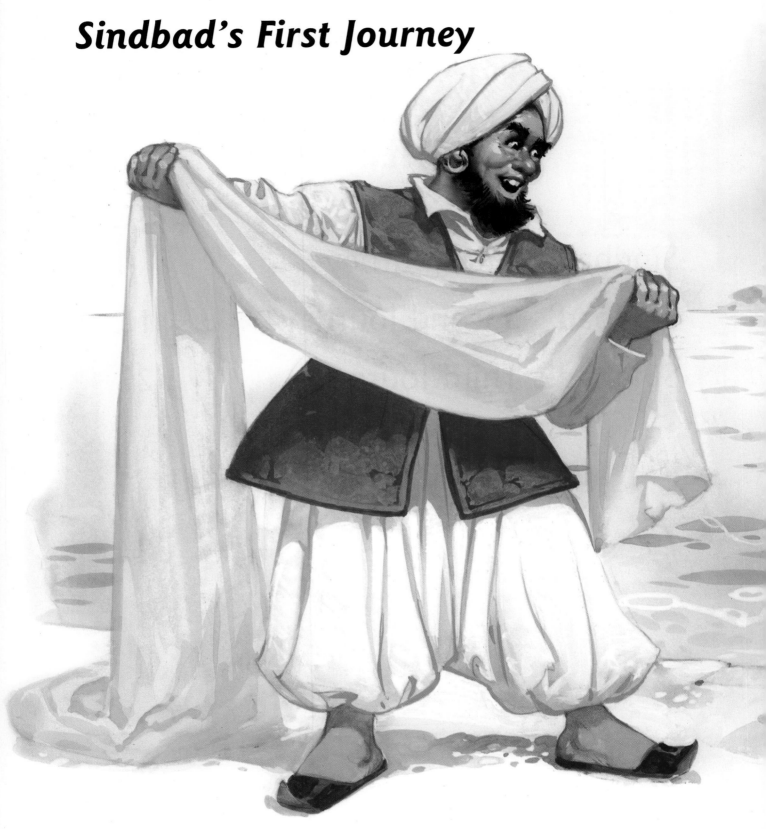

My name is Sindbad. I am a sailor.

I always wanted to be rich.

I make money by selling cloth, gold and spices in far-off countries.

One day, I had some beautiful cloth to sell.
'Can I come on your ship?' I said to a captain.
'Yes,' said the captain. 'We sail today.'

The ship sailed far, far away, stopping at many different islands.

I sold all my cloth and I made lots of money. I was very rich!

One day, I was on this beautiful island when …
CRASH! The island moved!

It was not an island, it was an enormous whale!
'Help!' I cried, jumping into the sea.

I was alone. I swam and swam.
I came to a little island where I found fruit
to eat and water to drink.

Many weeks went by. I saw nobody.

Then, one day, I had a surprise.
I saw a man on the beach.
'Oh, please help me,' I asked him.
'I'll take you to the king,' he said.

'Welcome,' said the king. 'I love to hear sailors' stories of far-off countries.'

I stayed. I told my stories and listened to others. One story began 'Once upon a time...'

'…We stopped on an island, but it wasn't an island.
It was a whale!'
'One sailor jumped into the sea. We never saw him again.
'That was me!' Sindbad cried.

11

'Sindbad!' the sailor cried. 'It's you!
We've got all your money on the ship.'

I thanked the king for his kindness and
sailed home, a rich man again.

Sindbad's Second Journey

Soon my money was gone. I sailed off, this time with spices to sell.

We stopped at a strange island and I fell asleep on the beach.

When I woke up, I was alone. The ship was gone!
I stood up. I could see something white, through the trees.
What WAS it? It looked ENORMOUS!

Suddenly, everything went dark. I looked up.
There was an enormous black bird – the Roc.
This must be where the Roc lived and the
enormous white thing was its egg.

'I can't stay here,' I thought.
I tied myself to the Roc's leg as it slept.
When it woke up, it took off, carrying me with it.

CRASH! We came down.
Where was I? There were no people anywhere.
All I could see were enormous rocks and diamonds.
I was by the diamond cave.

People cannot get into the cave. They get the diamonds out by throwing meat down onto them. Diamonds stick to the meat and the Roc flies out with it.

I was clever, too. I put diamonds in my pockets and tied
some meat to my chest. The Roc took the meat – and me –
and flew out of the cave.

The people at the top frightened the Roc with sticks. It let go of me.

'Thank you, everyone, for helping me get away,' I said. 'Here are some diamonds.'

The people happily took me to the nearest town from where I could sail home.

When I got home, I sold my diamonds. I was a rich man again!

Sindbad's Third Journey

I stayed at home for many years. I spent all my
money. Then I went away again.
This time I sailed far, far away with gold to sell.

Here, the waves were enormous.
The whales were enormous.
One whale opened its mouth to eat the ship.
'I'll be safer in the sea,' I thought.
I jumped in.

I was alone. I swam to a little island.
There were no people, but there were lots of trees.
I quickly made a raft from the wood and sailed off.

The waves were enormous. It was very dangerous.

After some weeks at sea, I finally saw some fishermen.
'Help!' I cried.
They pulled me and the raft from the sea.

One of the fishermen took me to his house.
He had a beautiful daughter.
'Can I marry her?' I asked him.
'You have no money,' he said and laughed.

'I'll sell my raft,' I said. 'It's made of very best wood. People will give gold for wood as good as this.'

I sold the raft. I was rich again.

'Do you love me?' I asked the fisherman's daughter.
'Yes, handsome sailor,' she said.
'And I'll marry you if you stay here and live with us.'
'I'll stay,' I said.

We lived very happily for many years. But, one day
I wanted to go back home. We still loved one another,
and my wife said she would come with me.

My friends were very surprised to see us.
'You've been on this journey for years!' they said.

'I know,' I laughed,
'but I'm home now.
I'm not going away again!'

Activities

Before you read

1. Look at the picture on the front of the book and also on page 4. What do you think the stories are about? Choose the best answer:
   a. A man who goes on one journey.
   b. A man who goes on three journeys.
   c. A man who stays at home.

2. These are all words that you will read in the stories. Match the words to the pictures. *Example*: (a) sailor

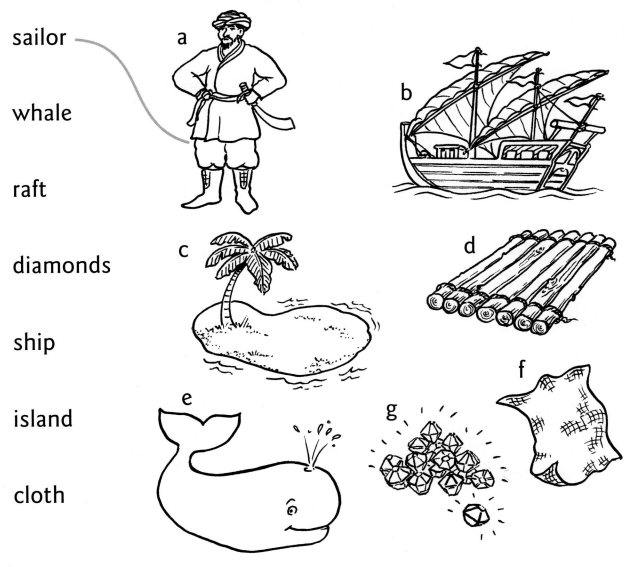

sailor

whale

raft

diamonds

ship

island

cloth

After you read

3. Can you match the words in the box below to the person who says them in the stories?

Example:
a. 'Can I come on your ship?'   *Sindbad*

b. 'We sail today.'
c. 'I'll take you to the king.'
d. 'Welcome.'
e. 'Sindbad, it's you!'
f. 'You have no money.'
g. 'Yes, handsome sailor.'
h. 'You've been on this journey for years!'

> Sindbad   Sindbad's friends   the captain
> the fisherman   the man on the beach
> the king   the sailor   the fisherman's daughter

4. Find the best words to complete each sentence.

Example:
a. Sindbad had ____*gold*____ to sell

b. There was _____ to cut.
c. There was _____ to eat.
d. There was _____ to drink.

> food   water   wood   gold

Answers to the Activities are published in the Penguin Young Readers Factsheets
on the website, www.penguinreaders.com